RECEIVING JESUS
for Little Ones

WRITTEN BY KIMBERLY FRIES

First Edition: February 2019

Cover by Sue Kouma Johnson

Illustrated by Kimberly Fries

ISBN-13: 9781795600071

Let the little children come to me;
do not hinder them;
for the kingdom of heaven
belongs to such as these.
- Mark 10:14

GO IN FRONT OF A CRUCIFIX OR THE BLESSED SACRAMENT.

Kneel down or sit in front of Jesus
and make the sign of the cross.

Call upon the Holy Spirit.

Come, Holy Spirit!

Set my heart on fire to receive Jesus,

to recognize his presence in the Eucharist,

and to share his life with everyone.

Soon you will receive Jesus in Holy Communion. Is your heart full of joy and excitement for such a special day?

CAN ANYONE RECEIVE JESUS INTO HIS
HEART AND NOT DIE OF HAPPINESS?

- BL. IMELDA LAMBERTINI

Have you wanted to see and talk to Jesus? God has something even greater in mind for you. You are going to receive his Body, Blood, Soul, and Divinity.

How many of you say: I should like to see His face, His garments, His shoes.

You do see Him.
You touch Him.
You eat Him.

He gives Himself to you, not only that you may see Him, but also to be your food and nourishment.

- St. John Chrysostom

Prepare to receive Jesus into your body and soul. Be sure to make a good confession and to fast an hour before you receive Holy Communion.

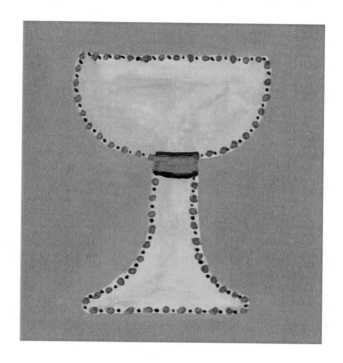

ON THIS EARTH, WHEN WE RECEIVE AN IMPORTANT PERSON, WE BRING OUT THE BEST-LIGHTS, MUSIC, FORMAL DRESS.

HOW SHOULD WE PREPARE TO RECEIVE CHRIST INTO OUR SOUL?

–ST. JOSEMARIA ESCRIVA

When you receive Jesus in the Eucharist, his love will change you forever. He is the Bread of Life, who will help you become a saint.

All the good that is in me is due to Holy Communion. I owe everything to it. I feel this holy fire has transformed me completely.

- St. Faustina

Here you are, a poor sinner on earth. Yet, God will visit you. Imagine being with Him forever in heaven, along with all the saints and angels.

THE EUCHARIST IS THE SUPREME PROOF
OF THE LOVE OF JESUS. AFTER THIS, THERE
IS NOTHING MORE BUT HEAVEN ITSELF.
- ST. PETER JULIAN EYMAR

What a miracle the Eucharist is! To receive God himself is such a privilege. Even the angels in heaven do not get to eat and drink the Son of God!

IF ANGELS COULD BE JEALOUS OF MEN,
THEY WOULD BE SO FOR ONE REASON:
HOLY COMMUNION.
– ST. MAXIMILIAN KOLBE

Once you have received Holy Communion, Jesus will be living in you. You will bring him everywhere you go. You will bring him to everyone you meet.

THE EUCHARIST IS THE SECRET OF MY DAY. IT GIVES STRENGTH AND MEANING TO ALL MY ACTIVITIES OF SERVICE TO THE CHURCH AND TO THE WHOLE WORLD.

– ST. JOHN PAUL II

After receiving Jesus, tell him how much you love him. Thank him for all of the blessings that he has given you and for the gift of himself in Holy Communion.

Prayer After Communion

I thank you, Lord, Almighty Father, Everlasting God, for having been pleased through no merit of mine, but of Your great mercy alone, to feed me, a sinner, and Your unworthy servant, with the precious Body and Blood of Your Son, our Lord Jesus Christ.

- St. Thomas Aquinas

Most importantly, close your eyes, and have a quiet moment in your heart with Jesus. Remember his love for you and know that you are completely united with him.

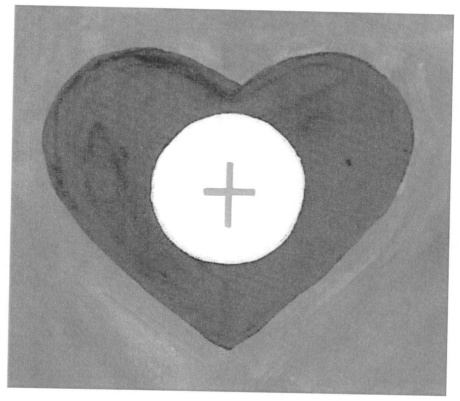

WHEN YOU HAVE RECEIVED HOLY
COMMUNION, CLOSE YOUR BODILY
EYES SO THAT YOU MAY OPEN THE EYES
OF YOUR SOUL. THEN LOOK UPON
JESUS IN THE CENTER OF YOUR HEART.

- ST. TERESA OF AVILA

If you want to become a saint with Jesus forever, go to Holy Communion often. Keep your soul pure by going to confession and prayerfully prepare for Mass. Also, visit Jesus often in the Blessed Sacrament.

I CAN NO LONGER LIVE WITHOUT JESUS.
HOW SOON SHALL I RECEIVE HIM AGAIN?

- ST. MARIA GORETTI

I love you Jesus!

I love you Mary!

Thank you for the beautiful gift

of the Eucharist!

MAKE THE
SIGN OF THE CROSS.

COLLECT THEM ALL

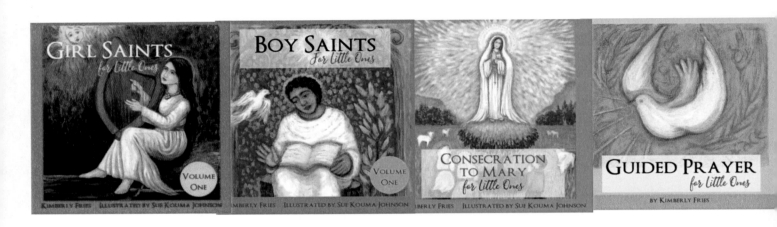

Meet the Author

I'm Kimberly Fries, homeschooling mom and author. I live in North Dakota with my husband and three children. Creating Catholic books to help children develop a personal relationship with God, Mary, and the saints has been such a joy for me. I pray that my books greatly bless your family and assist you in your journey to become saints!

I would love to hear from you!

Please write a review at Amazon.com.

Want to be the first to know about my new releases?

Follow me on Facebook, Instagram, Youtube, and my blog!
www.mylittlenazareth.com

Interested in getting wholesale prices?

E-mail me at mylittlenazareth@gmail.com

33804835R00018

Made in the USA
San Bernardino, CA
26 April 2019